Chris Howkins' Tow-path Book

Published by Chris Howkins
1983

By
Pyrford Lock
29-10-1982

First Published 1983
© Copyright Christopher Howkins 1983.

CHRISTOPHER HOWKINS, 70 GRANGE ROAD, NEW HAW, WEYBRIDGE, SURREY, KT15 3RH.

Printed in England
by Alderson Brothers
(Printers) Ltd.,
Hersham, Surrey.

ISBN 0 9509105 0 3

Tow-path Book

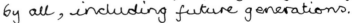

Lapwings

INTRODUCTION:

Woodlouse

Imagine some water meadows under a black winter sky about to storm, with a very low sun lighting the oaks in greenish gold and the birches in reddish purple, all contrasting sharply with the winter emerald of the grass. If you were really there you would even smell it and hear the Lapwing calls shredding in the wind. I cannot draw all that though. Some pictures are for the heart only.

What this book does contain is a selection of my notes, sketches and drawings relating to what can be seen when walking the tow-path of the Wey and Godalming Navigations in Surrey. This stretches nearly twenty miles through historic areas and beautiful countryside. To squash all that into ninety six pages is even more taxing than even I imagined when I began! Consequently, some people will be disappointed that their favourite spot has been omitted but hopefully they will find fresh interests too. If this book enhances peoples' appreciation just a little bit it will have served well.

Please remember that the Navigations and their tow-path belong to the National Trust but the adjoining lands are private and should be respected as such. Similarly, please observe the National Trust Byelaws so that this property may be enjoyed by all, including future generations.

By Send Church.

This property is currently costing the National Trust some £500 per acre to maintain. This they are only just able to raise from boat licences etc.

The National Trust Navigation Office is at Dapdune Lea, Wharf Road, Guildford. Phone Guildford 61389.

3.

By popular demand the format of this book follows that used in its predecessor 'The Doorstep Book'. Any differences are hopefully improvements.

As requested, there are more sketches and fewer finished drawings in this book. There are nearly 200 of them of which only nine have been previously published. Nearly all have been sketched on the spot, even if finished off in the studio. Where photographs have been used they have been my own so that the vision is still mine.

Send.

The information has been collected over a number of years and most of it orally. It has sometimes been difficult to check but is accurate to the best of my knowledge. I suspect that versions of some stories will always remain contradictory.

TERMS

Some people would prefer me to use "towing-path" rather than "tow-path". Surrey folk seem to use tow-path and I have done the same. Both words are listed in the Oxford English Dictionary.

Strictly speaking the waterway is a "navigation" and not a "canal" because it is not entirely man-made. It is a river made navigable. I have used canal throughout because it is easier and because again that is what Surrey folk call it. Which parts are river and which parts are canal is best decided from looking at the Ordnance Survey maps. This is often claimed to be the earliest canal still in use in England. That is very debatable. How much does a river need to be modified to be considered? Do you include the navigable drainage channels of the Fens? It is generally agreed that the earliest true canal is the Bridgewater Canal of 1761.

CHANGES

During the preparation of this manuscript it has been necessary to alter several sections because of changes. Other places have been marked with a footnote. So get your cameras, sketch pads and tape recorders and make a record of our rapidly changing scene and of people's memories.

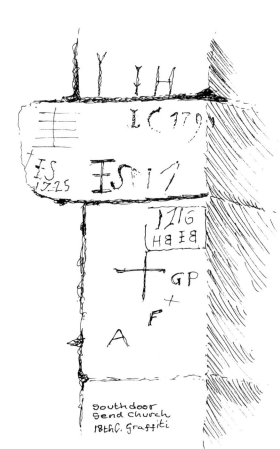

Southdoor
Send Church
18th C. Graffiti

MAPS

A sketch map has not been included because to really appreciate where you are, all the detail of an Ordnance Survey map is needed.

Maps 186 and 187 of the 1:50 000 First Series are required. The 187 begins at Weybridge and misses the first mile or so of the canal. For that the 176 is required. The 186 and 187 meet at Walsham Gates.

SEQUENCE

After the first few pages of general background information the book is divided into short sections covering the ground between locks.

HISTORY

This is not intended as a history of the waterway so do not look for such a section. Pieces of history have been worked in where it seemed that such would add to your appreciation of the walk.

The landscape itself, with all that is in it, is the history book we need if we can learn how to read it — not a stuffy old book but a lively one for which there has not been time enough to finish.

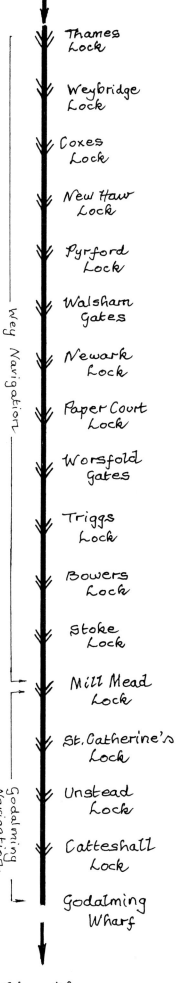

River Thames

Thames Lock

Weybridge Lock

Coxes Lock

New Haw Lock

Pyrford Lock

Walsham Gates

Newark Lock

Paper Court Lock

Worsfold Gates

Triggs Lock

Bowers Lock

Stoke Lock

Wey Navigation

Mill Mead Lock

St. Catherine's Lock

Unstead Lock

Catteshall Lock

Godalming Navigation

Godalming Wharf

River Wey

SIR RICHARD WESTON
AND THE FOUNDING OF
THE WEY NAVIGATION.

The creative force behind the scheme was Sir Richard Weston, variously described as "active and public spirited" or as "delinquent". His is a fascinating story, of a teenager with ideas who energetically began executing them in his early twenties but was then thwarted for thirty years, only to die months before his canal was finally opened. For Weston they were difficult times. He wished to follow the Roman Catholic faith but the country was officially Protestant. He was considered Royalist but the King was deposed. He had problems.

In 1521 Henry VIII granted the Manor of Sutton, near Guildford, to the Westons. One Sir Richard Weston (died 1542) began building his country house, Sutton Place, in 1523-5. In so doing he created an important house in the history of English architecture.

In 1591 our Sir Richard was born, into times made stable by the Tudor régime. He was able to travel abroad and did so with an alert eye for ways of improving land and making it profitable. He became the owner of Sutton Place in 1613 and set about implementing his ideas on his estates. He is credited with introducing turnpikes but more important were ideas for waterways, brought back from the Low Countries. Commercially he was interested in irrigation channels. Scenically he built tumbling bays :- barriers of boulders set diagonally across the river over which the water would tumble attractively. He is also credited (probably wrongly) with introducing pound locks. Certainly he built the first one in Surrey, at Stoke, about 1618. He foresaw the option of charging tolls on the river craft wishing to short-cut across his estates and thus began the long struggle to canalise the whole river from Guildford downwards.

Eventually Charles I approved the scheme and appointed Sir Richard as a Commissioner. Thus he was seen as a Royalist, at a time when that was dangerous and a disadvantage when funds had to be raised. He resorted to selling off the family lands at Clandon and Merrow. These had been emparked by licence by charter on May 25th 1530. Now, 1641, Temple House (not the Manor) was sold to Sir Richard Onslow to become Clandon Park.

Above: costume sketches, not portraits.

Sir Richard Weston's arms

This may have been a diplomatic move as Onslow was an important Parliamentarian. The next year Civil War broke out. Sir Richard's estates were sequestered and he went into exile in Europe.

Another interesting Parliamentarian comes into the story: Major James Pitson, Commissioner for Surrey. He successfully arbitrated for the pardon of Weston and for the return of his estates. He was a dangerous ally, generating floods of accusations about double dealings and unscrupulous activities.

Weston trod carefully. He wrote "Directions for the Improvement of Barren Land" (1645, 1651 & 1652). It's forgotten now, including his advocacy of growing turnips for winter feed. Instead we credit Viscount 'Turnip' Townsend with the idea but he came fifty years later. The idea of growing clover to enrich the soil and hay was another of Weston's ideas, brought back from Brabant and Flanders. We still call the white clover "Dutch" clover. Sainfoin too is credited to him but is possibly a native so let's say he drew attention to its value.

1650 brought another step forward. The former royal Palace of Oatlands at Weybridge was demolished, as a condition of sale by Parliament. To recoup his money, the new owner, Robert Turbridge, sold off the materials. These Weston bought for constructing the locks. The timbers have mostly been replaced. The Tudor bricks hide behind modern facings but a large dressed stone is clearly visible on the corner of Stoke Lock.

This sudden activity was possible because 'The Long Parliament' passed the Act for "making the Wey Navigable", on June 26th 1651. The Act had been introduced on December 26th previously. Sir Richard overcame the Royalist problem by invoking the active support of the town of Guildford. The town was in commercial decline, especially the wool trade, but an improved transport system might reverse matters, so the Act was presented in their name.

On May 7th 1652 Sir Richard Weston died. The family chapel was in the vestry of Holy Trinity, Guildford. It had been founded by the ancestor who built Sutton Place. So Sir Richard only saw the first ten miles of his scheme. Four more remained. His son George took over and the canal opened the following year but the problems were only just beginning.

. . . .

George Weston was one of fourteen sons. He had several sisters too. Their mother was Grace Harper from Cheshunt. George and brother John had been married by their father to the granddaughters of William Copley. Sir Richard was acting as their guardian at the time because his friend Copley had lost his lands to the Parliamentarians for his Roman Catholic faith. Copley took a dim view of the marriages.

Sainfoin

Dutch Clover.

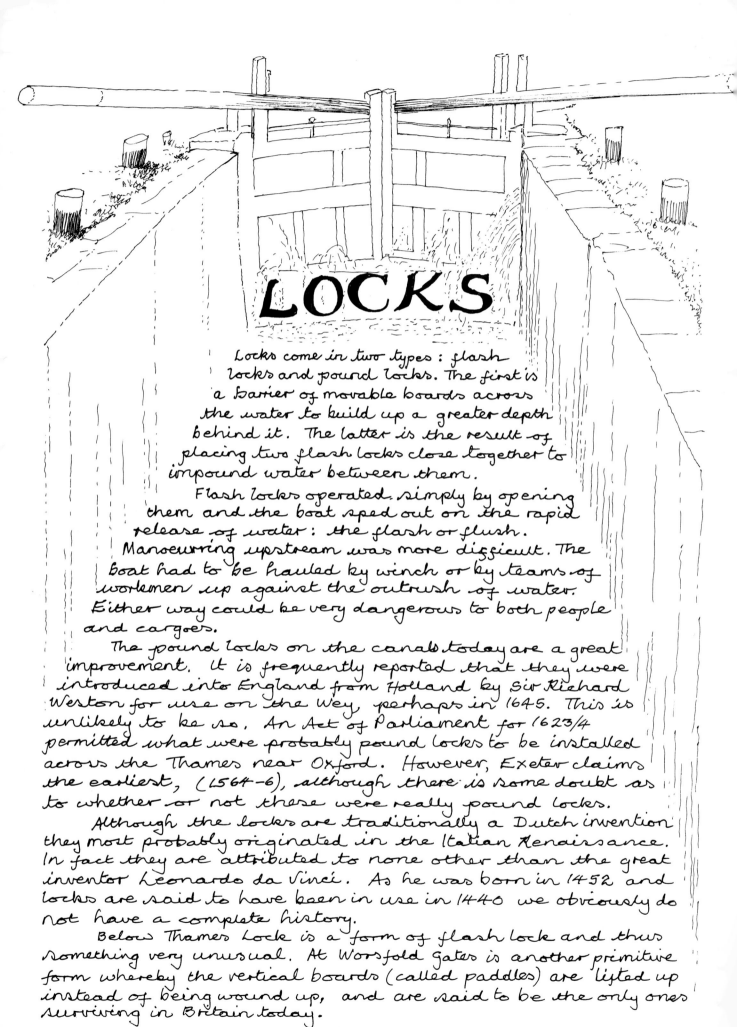

LOCKS

Locks come in two types: flash locks and pound locks. The first is a barrier of movable boards across the water to build up a greater depth behind it. The latter is the result of placing two flash locks close together to impound water between them.

Flash locks operated simply by opening them and the boat sped out on the rapid release of water: the flash or flush. Manoeuvring upstream was more difficult. The boat had to be hauled by winch or by teams of workmen up against the outrush of water. Either way could be very dangerous to both people and cargoes.

The pound locks on the canals today are a great improvement. It is frequently reported that they were introduced into England from Holland by Sir Richard Weston for use on the Wey, perhaps in 1645. This is unlikely to be so. An Act of Parliament for 1623/4 permitted what were probably pound locks to be installed across the Thames near Oxford. However, Exeter claims the earliest, (1564-6), although there is some doubt as to whether or not these were really pound locks.

Although the locks are traditionally a Dutch invention they most probably originated in the Italian Renaissance. In fact they are attributed to none other than the great inventor Leonardo da Vinci. As he was born in 1452 and locks are said to have been in use in 1440 we obviously do not have a complete history.

Below Thames Lock is a form of flash lock and thus something very unusual. At Worsfold Gates is another primitive form whereby the vertical boards (called paddles) are lifted up instead of being wound up, and are said to be the only ones surviving in Britain today.

Design: Thames Lock

Barges

Modern barge passing through the flash Lock at Weybridge.
January 1983

Of the many types of craft to be seen on the canal, the barges are the broad-beamed freight vessels. To call any other craft a barge is an insult, an unfortunate one if you say it to the face of a proud narrow-boat owner.

Barges are undecorated. They are also popularly believed to be devoid of living quarters. This is not always the case. As the men may have been away for as much as a month living quarters were squeezed into the ends. I have been shown photographs of some very attractive cabins.

The last establishment to employ barges on the Wey was Coxes Lock Mill at Addlestone. Their use was discontinued in 1969 but revived again in 1981 until the Mill closed in 1983. The barge sketched above was returning from the mill.

The last barge to be actually built on the Wey was "Perseverance III". This was rebuilt during 1964-5 at Dapdune Wharf, Guildford and made its last journey in 1968. There is a scale model of it in Guildford Museum.

Some of the barges carried 80 tons or even 95 on some occasions. Hauling these by horse power is a popular image but this declined during the 19thC. in favour of man power. Such men were called 'bow-haulers' because the tow-rope was fixed to the bow. However, local pronunciation makes it rhyme with 'tow' and the syllables are run together to sound more like 'bowlers'. Sometimes only one man was used, sometimes a team. It depended upon the conditions. Some were men from the barges; some were workers on the river. They shifted a barge as fast as could a horse.

Barges leaving Guildford at four or
five o'clock in the morning expected to
be at Weybridge by four o'clock in the
afternoon. That is, in time to bring
back a return load. Sometimes horses
would be taken direct to Weybridge by
road to save time, in order to be sure
of getting the load. No load - no money

The barges were also moved with
punting poles, oars and sails. It
was always a highly skilled job. The
Wey barges were usually about 72 feet
long and 14 feet wide : a superb
battering ram! I've been entertained
these last few months with quite a number
of disaster stories, featuring rammings
and sinkings. Floods increased the
hazards of course but so did strong
winds. Sometimes a donkey or pony would
be used at the stern to prevent it
swinging out.

Quick study of bow-
haulers from an old
photograph kindly lent
for the purpose.

"Poling"
From a photograph kindly lent
by J.C.M. Blatch Esq.

11.

SAILING BARGES

Eric Parker's "Highways and Byeways in Surrey" (1908) has an illustration of a sailing barge at Weybridge. I wondered how something as massive as a sailing barge could get up the canal to Eastwood's wharf at Town Bridge. I found an answer by sheer and glorious luck!

A Wey sailing barge from an old photograph kindly lent for the purpose. It was very worn so the sketch is only an impression. The other photographs available were not free of copyright for me to use.

Eastwood's needed to get bricks from their works in Kent and Essex, so in 1903 they had two "stumpy spritsail" barges made for them at Sittingbourne. These were to be small enough to fit the canal. At least, that was the idea but "Surrey" would only fit if one leeboard was removed and stowed on deck. I'm told this is what is showing in my sketch. It doesn't show in the drawing made by Hugh Thomson for Parker's book so he must have come upon the smaller "Landrail".

Some of the main Wey barges had sails too. These were kept mainly for use on the Thames part of their journeys, due to all the little low bridges over the canal. They had a capacity of 65 tons but only bore 45 tons to Guildford due to the weight of the sails etc. They sailed up the Basingstoke Canal to Woking too. The sails were red.

TUGS

After their invention, steam tugs were used to haul the barges up the Thames from London Docks to Putney, Teddington, etc. from where they proceeded in the traditional manner. One tug could tow six barges. The "Teddington" hauled grain barges right up to Coxes Lock Mill and "Oasis" went all the way up to Guildford.

CARGOES

Corn and flour exchanging at Coxes Lock Mill were the most important cargoes. Timber probably came second, with several timber yards along the canal. Moon's at Guildford still operates. Then came vital supplies such as coal, sugar, groceries, maize and barley together with raw materials such as bark for tanning, rags for paper, kapok, linseed, monkey nuts and chalk. Gunpowder from mills at Chilworth was the most specialised cargo, until 1920.

NARROW BOATS

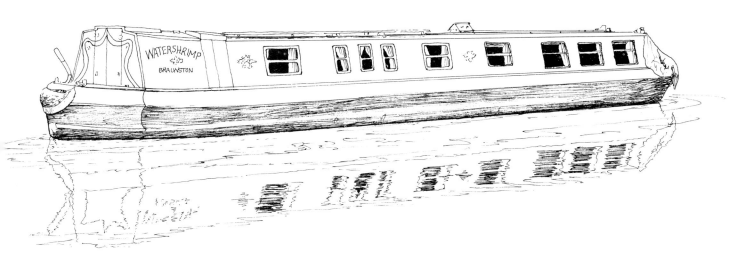

Early in the 19th C. evolved craft which we call narrow boats. They have distinctive regional variations totalling several hundred so 'boat spotting' is a highly skilled enthusiasm. I was surprised to hear that these boats are entirely British and not to be found on the Continent.

Another thing I was told, very firmly, was not to call them long boats as some people do. Long boats are Viking ships and modern boat people are not bent on rape and pillage. I was told that very firmly too!

Narrow boats worked in pairs: motor and butty, each weighing about 25 tons. Although only six or seven feet wide they are some seventy feet long so they can carry large amounts in the central holds. Just enough space is left on the motor for the engine room and for the living space back on the butty. The living space was only about six feet by eight feet and yet whole families grew up there. Nowadays the holds are converted into living space so that the craft can become house boats or serve the holiday trade.

One such boat is the 'Watershrimp' which returns to Braunston each summer to earn its keep on holiday tours but during the winter it's back on the Wey working as a superb little restaurant, seating twelve. Swans peer in from one side while marsh tits feed at the bird table outside the opposite window. It is owned and managed by Mr and Mrs Shrimpton; both very enthusiastic and very welcoming.

THE FIRST BOATS on the canal
have gone unrecorded but the idea came from Holland, where, in the 17th C. the artists were busy recording everyday life. They show us what ideas were brought back: rowing boats and broad boats with sails.

THAMES LOCK
TO
WEYBRIDGE LOCK

Map 176 : 072655
to 187 : 069648

Path Condition :
usually very good.

"*Path Condition* : usually very good" means the path can be usually walked in ordinary shoes. Hazards are given where necessary. Throughout its length it is clear to follow. Until Walsham it runs over sand which drains well (apart from ruts) but then it becomes clay.

From the town, Thames Street, Weybridge, leads down to a wide pool in the Thames. Here, by D'Oyly Carte Island, Shepperton Weir provides a favourite testing place for young canoeists. The island is where Rupert D'Oyly Carte brought his Savoy Operatic Company for meetings and rehearsals. It was his father's, bought with the intention of using it for an extension of his Savoy Hotel but his idea didn't appeal to the licensing authorities.

The quiet backwater through the trees on the left of the sketch above wouldn't be recognised as the entrance to the Wey Navigation if it wasn't for a large notice.

The tow-path is reached down an alley beside The Old Crown just up the street past the boatyard. There were wharves here even in medieval times and the Tudor Palace of Oatlands stood a little further back on higher ground. During the Commonwealth when Crown property was in the hands of Parliament, the Palace of Oatlands was sold off to Robert Turbridge on condition that he destroy it. This he did to recoup his outlay by selling off the building materials. Thus they ended up in the canal locks. Nowadays most are concealed behind modern facings.

The footpath arrives at Thames Lock and crosses it by an arched wooden footbridge. This gives good views down into the lock to watch it working. From here can also be seen, downstream, the single gate acting as a flash lock, (right). This raises the water level sufficiently to allow craft to pass that need an extra two and a half feet or so to clear the bottom cill. These occasions arise when the Thames is low or when heavily laden craft use the canal. The latter still applies now that commercial grain barges once again serve Coxes Lock Mill, a mile upstream.

The industrial building above the lock is Thames Lock Mill, one of over forty mills which have been sited along the River Wey. This high number results from the river having a very constant flow due to its many sources being very widely separated in both the chalk and sandstone hills to the south. The disadvantage is the risk of flooding when the river is impeded by locks, so overflows were created at regular intervals. This is the first and on the island it created a mill was built by 1693. It made paper. By 1720 it had been converted to the more profitable business of working the local iron from mines on nearby St. George's Hill. When that ran out (1817) it became derelict until rebuilt for oil seed crushing in 1842. (see next page).

Leaving the lock the tow-path passes moored boats and then has another overflow beside it, called The Bulldogs. Here and on the other bank the trees are close. There are glimpses of fields. Kingfishers can be spotted and I've even flushed out a woodcock. It all seems so rural yet it's right beside Weybridge town centre.

Young canoeists.
Shepperton Weir
14·11·1981

15.

The Fireman's Tale

'At about eleven o'clock on Monday night, December 24th, a tremendous fire broke out at the Weybridge Oil Mills owned by Mr. Nias. The mills, which were built on an island close to the spot where the rivers Thames and Wey meet, are of considerable extent, both steam and water power being used. The fire apparently originated at the wharf on the Wey, and rapidly reached the warehouse where several tons of linseed were stored. It next caught the engine house and adjoining shed where over forty tons of cakes were waiting to be sent off by barges. Fears were now entertained for the safety of the refining shed which contained several vats of linseed oil in various stages of manufacture. Between this shed and parts of the building on fire, several casks of oil had been standing. These were rolled into the river for safety.

A strong wind now set in and the refining shed caught fire. In a very short time one of the vats burst, and the oil flowed down, a real stream of fire, into the River Wey, and ignited the casks of oil which had been placed in the water for safety. The scene was now awfully grand. Flames rose from the water higher than the fourth storey of the mill. As vat after vat inside burst and sent forth its share to the conflagration, the scene increased in its terrible grandeur.........'

From 'The Fireman' 15th January 1878. Courtesy of Weybridge Museum.
Illustration: Thames Lock Mill 1976.

16.

WEYBRIDGE

-Road.

When those horse-drawn fire-engines galloped through that Christmas night, from Byfleet, Staines and Walton, they entered a very different Weybridge from today. Streets we think of as old were then new. The old village street was changing. All around there was new building. A small town was rapidly developing as a direct result of the arrival of the railway in 1838. It brought the possibility of working in the City but living in the country. Thus Weybridge attracted a new stratum to its society. This is the visual story one sees on walking the streets today, perhaps a little surprised that a town so small should be so widely known. The development has been so overwhelming that even the old core has gone. The parish church had to be rebuilt, in 1848, to cope with changes in both population and in current taste as to what a 'decent' church should be.

Above: Radnor Road 1982

H. 29·10·82

It was this Earl who bought a
large amount of shares in the
canal in 1723. He and his
descendants, together with the
Langton family from Lincolnshire
controlled the canal for over a
hundred years. The 2nd and 3rd
Earls ran into many problems.
By 1793 it was necessary for the
Chief Justices and Barons to
appoint two additional trustees
but these were related to the
Portmore family. It was not
a happy time for the canal.

From Weybridge Lock the tow-path
immediately introduces all the
variety of its journey despite being so
close to town centre.

Trees border the canal with
fields beyond. There is a good
selection of Britain's waterside
flora and a good selection of
birds from House sparrows to
woodcock. There are backwaters
and weirs; boats and people
and quiet times too.

Young grey squirrel.
1980

H. 1980

The land beyond the canal was
once Portmore Park created in the
1670's by the 6th Duke of Norfolk,
Henry Howard. It was set out by
1678 when John Evelyn, the diarist,
visited.

The Duke's widow sold it
in 1688 to King James II who gave
it to Catherine Sedley, Countess
of Dorchester, who had once been
his mistress. She married Sir
David Colyear: a Scottish soldier
under William III who raised him
to Baron (1699) and then Earl of
Portmore in 1703. He died in 1729.

The land on the tow-path side
Hamm Court, has a history going
back to the early middle ages. In
1732 it became part of the Portmore
estates when the 2nd Earl leased
it from the Dean and Canons of
St. George's Windsor. The house
became derelict.

The 3rd Earl, the 'bad old Earl'
disregarded the estate completely
to spite his heir with whom
he had quarrelled. Thus in
1834 the Dean and Canons
refused the renew the lease
for the 4th Earl.

Nothing remains
of these two country houses,
except the moat and well at
Hamm Court* and a pair of gate
piers re-erected at the end of
Portmore Park Road.

*Private property

Soon a bridge comes into view. This was begun in 1939 but had to wait until after the war for completion.

The tow-path goes under it and then turns right, past a weather boarded building, left up a track to the road and rejoins the canal.

The road crosses the water by an iron bridge dating from 1865. Between the two bridges is a wide pool beside the old wharf. The River Wey comes in under the iron bridge with the canal sneaking in through an arch in its abutment; shown in the sketch below (reprinted from the Doorstep Book).

Acheulian Hand-Axe from the ford; courtesy of Weybridge Museum.

G.H. 1981

TOWPATH

Although bridges were constructed since early medieval times there was always a need for the ford: carts were too wide to use the bridge. A bridge referred to in 1571 was only just over five feet wide. That wasn't rebuilt until 1808 and even then its replacement was still of wood, until iron was used.

Toad on the road. 1975

This has been a crossing place since man first came to the valley. Here Bronze Age Man lost his weapons. They are now in Weybridge Museum. Later a bridge was constructed and gave its name to the settlement which grew up here: Weybridge.

WEYBRIDGE LOCK
TO
COXES LOCK

O.S. Map 187 068647 to 061641

Path condition : usually very good

After trudging around Weybridge pavements this stretch provides
the grand feeling of earth and grass beneath your feet. For many,
though, the least attractive or interesting stretch of the whole
tow-path but wherever I've brought children s' drawing groups
here we've always found something to capture our imaginations.
There's a round house and an old channel full of rotting boats,
deep enough for the yellow water lilies (below) and for the
fluffy cygnets (opposite) to learn their foraging skills. Now
that the adjacent gravel pit has been infilled the bird life
is very noticeably reduced. The flora is rather limited here
too.

Preening contortions:
Mute Swan
Weybridge Lock; 5·9·1977

It is arguable whether the Mute Swan, Cygnus olor, is an introduced species or not. Its documented history goes right back to the early Middle Ages and an Act of Parliament of 1483 restricted swan ownership to those whose estates were valued at five marks. Even today the unmarked swans belong to the Crown. Marked swans belong to two of the City of London's Livery Companies: those with one notch in their beak to the Dyers' Company and those with two notches to the Vintners' Company.

The Yellow Water-lily (left) is a beautiful native but beware of close inspection for deep water lurks beneath the floating spread of leaves. Their stems often rise 2 m. from the bottom, occasionally 3 m. The canal of course is not as deep as that.

The flowers smell of alcohol which attracts small flies for pollination. Probably it is not so much the scent as the shape of the fruits which has earned it the country name of Brandy Bottle Plant.

Just as folk medicine sets great store in having a drop of brandy in the back of the cupboard, so many virtues have been found in this plant, especially in the roots. A range of active constituents is found there, especially nuphar-tannic acid. It has been recommended for an even wider range of disorders, such as diarrhoea, boils, ulcers, and inflamations. Do not experiment with it!

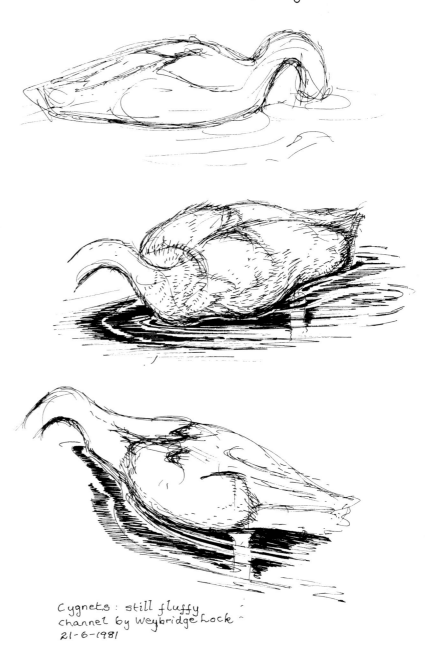

Cygnets: still fluffy channel by Weybridge Lock - 21-6-1981

* Since making the above sketch the industrial site has been rebuilt.

14·7·1978

When the days begin to lengthen there's the welcome return of chances to sketch quickly after work, as the nightly shadows seem to ooze out of the very ground, when the colours are rich and dark or lightly catching the last of the sun, when the sky is pale turquoise and the water icy silver, yet the reeds push up new growth as their assurance that spring is coming.

On such an evening I recorded Coxes Lock Mill and the edge of the Industrial Estate (above) from Black Boy Bridge ~ named after a garden statue I'm told.

Left: Moorhen fleeing in panic; field sketch.

Moorhens don't like artists. Human beings are supposed to keep moving. Those that do not must be watched, preferably from the thickest vegetation available.

@Hawkins.

The canal in different mood: on one of those endless sunny summer days when it's too hot to do anything more than sit around. If you need an excuse then fishing or drawing serve very well!

The view above shows the boats and factories shown in the scene opposite but looking back in the other direction. It was drawn from below the railway bridge, built for the branch line from Weybridge to Chertsey, opened in 1848. It was extended to join the main line at Virginia Water in 1865-6.

Scene above reproduced with kind permission of their parents.

12·6·77

23.

For some reason, people quite like watermills. They obstruct our waterways with their industrial bulk yet we don't mind. Coxes Lock Mill is no exception. On a sunny day there are always people here: boaters and walkers, artists and fishermen and people just enjoying the sunshine. Very imposing the mill is too, especially as it is still working full time and uses the canal as a highway again. Its Georgian appearance is misleading as it was rebuilt at the beginning of this century. Then in the mid-1960s the giant wheat silo was added (137 feet high) and in 1969 the smaller flour silo was built. There has been a mill here for over two hundred years though. The water power was superceded by steam and that by electricity. Today it is one of twenty two mills run by Allied Mills Ltd., producing 60 tonnes of flour per day.

The corn is not ground into flour but stripped from the husks by fluted steel rollers, a Swiss invention. Inside the mill are some of the most modern milling machines in Britain and again they are Swiss. By contrast there are also some of the oldest working machines. It's all

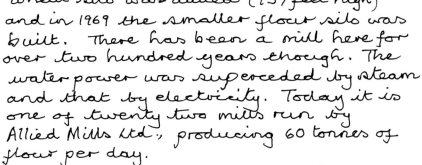

CH. 1975

very quiet and very, very clean.

Until 1829 Coxes Lock Mill worked iron and then changed hands to become a flour mill. At this time an inventory of contents was made which included items likely to substantiate the tradition that silk was spun here. We don't know who spun it or exactly when.

Before the mill was built King James I wanted to rear silkworms at Oatlands Palace, Weybridge but he was sent black mulberries in error. Silkworms eat white mulberries!

N.B. Coxes Lock Mill closed down April 1983 after this section of the manuscript was completed.

Wren studies.
Actual size from the sketchbook.

They don't stay still for more than a couple of seconds!

13·5·1980

Quick sketch between storms!

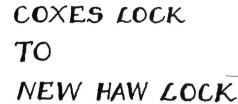

COXES LOCK
TO
NEW HAW LOCK

Map 187 : 061641 to 055630

Path condition : Usually very good;
            a few damp ruts to skip.

Beside Coxes Lock is the mill pond but when it was created isn't clear. There is a land settlement document dated 1783 but this may not be the actual site. Another document would lead us to believe that the mill was opened in 1789 but this is contradicted by another reference, to iron hoops being made, in 1770. Let's just say it belongs to the second half of the eighteenth century! Originally the mill pond was smaller.

The best time to see the pond is on a clear winter's afternoon when a red sun hangs just over the water, stark behind the black silhouettes of the alder trees on the intervening embankment between the canal and the pond. (Above)

It is a good place for birds, especially the Coot and the Great Crested Grebe. Both are scarce on anything but open water. The mill pond provides that but the canal does not. The familiar swan we take for granted but compare its map of distribution with that of the coot and its range is seen to be quite limited. We are lucky to have it and that it should be so familiar.

Part of the
mill pond and canal
from the mill wheat silo.*
Detail from a larger drawing.

* Planning permission being
sought for the demolition
of the silo.

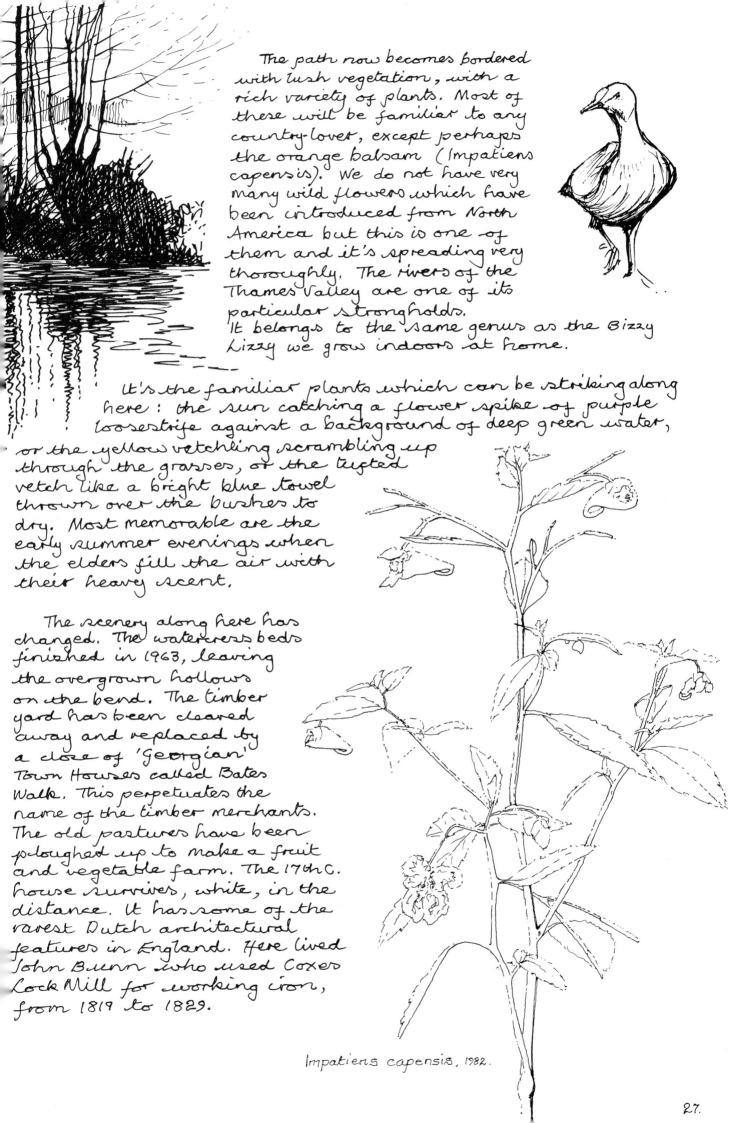

The path now becomes bordered with lush vegetation, with a rich variety of plants. Most of these will be familiar to any country-lover, except perhaps the orange balsam (Impatiens capensis). We do not have very many wild flowers which have been introduced from North America but this is one of them and it's spreading very thoroughly. The rivers of the Thames Valley are one of its particular strongholds.
It belongs to the same genus as the Bizzy Lizzy we grow indoors at home.

It's the familiar plants which can be striking along here: the sun catching a flower spike of purple loosestrife against a background of deep green water, or the yellow vetchling scrambling up through the grasses, or the tufted vetch like a bright blue towel thrown over the bushes to dry. Most memorable are the early summer evenings when the elders fill the air with their heavy scent.

The scenery along here has changed. The watercress beds finished in 1963, leaving the overgrown hollows on the bend. The timber yard has been cleared away and replaced by a close of 'Georgian' Town Houses called Bates Walk. This perpetuates the name of the timber merchants. The old pastures have been ploughed up to make a fruit and vegetable farm. The 17th C. house survives, white, in the distance. It has some of the rarest Dutch architectural features in England. Here lived John Bunn who used Coxes Lock Mill for working iron, from 1819 to 1829.

Impatiens capensis, 1982.

NEW HAW LOCK
TO
PYRFORD LOCK

During Restoration.

At New Haw lock stands one of the old lock cottages: a Listed Building of the 1780's. A gas cylinder explosion in 1982 caused extensive damage (some £12,000 worth) but after five months of restoration it was saved and handed back to the National Trust. It is an important element in the landscape for here there is so little to illustrate the continuity of our culture, unless of course the fair is in the adjoining field. This is not an easy place to go sketching (see opposite) and neither is the new M25 viaduct an easy subject. Fresh pale concrete doesn't look right in black ink. Overleaf are three quick sketches, actual size, made during its construction in 1982, and superimposed upon a finished drawing. (reproduced page 30).

Horse-power and helmets and
trials of skill to attract a
female; knights and squires
and teenagers; perhaps fairs
haven't changed so much
after all!

Fair At New Haw.

NEW HAW VIADUCT

C Hawkins
20·8·1982

Next, of interest, is the junction with the Basingstoke Canal (above) which was opened in 1796. It's much longer than the Wey Navigation, extending thirty seven miles to Basingstoke via Woking and Aldershot. Originally it was important for bringing farm produce from rural Hampshire to the London food markets, until the railways could do it better. Even then the canal did not die completely. Until 1921 it was used regularly for supplying the army camps at Aldershot. The first stretch, to Woking, was kept in use until 1949 by the Woking Gas Works. Subsequently it has become derelict and the usable stretch from this junction extends only about 500 yds to Woodham Bottom Lock. However, it is currently being restored and should re-open soon. Perhaps then, the footbridge which once linked the two tow-paths will be replaced.

The railway bridge over the canal at this point opened in 1838, carrying the London and South Western Railway towards Southampton. Nowadays it runs into Waterloo but that terminus was not opened until 1848. Previously the line had terminated at Nine Elms, where there was a vast area of marshalling yards, locomotive sheds and riverside wharves. London, unlike most European cities, had separate terminals for freight and passengers. The story turns back on itself with the move of Covent Garden Market out to Nine Elms.

Boathouses, bridge, mill and house make an interesting spot ahead. Part of the old Parvis Bridge dates from 1760 and blocks the route of the tow-path so that the road has to be crossed. There is a new bridge too, spanning the M25, and where the path rejoins the canal is an old "shed". This is the last relic of days when there was a cottage and several buildings along the bank here, which acted as the wharf for nearby Byfleet. It is an old grist mill for which the date 1780 has been suggested to me. It was working well into living memory.

Opposite, through the trees, is West Hall. At the end of last century it was bought by a Dutchman named Stoops. He had two boat-houses built where the canal had been built wider for turning boats. One still functions as such. The other was converted into a private home after the last war. It stands opposite. As boathouses there were social distinctions to be observed and the existing boathouse was the more lowly one. People still remember when regattas were held here.

Surrey Grist Mill, with tow-path
Parvis Bridge, Byfleet.

I would much rather have seen the bicycle race in the grounds of West Hall but that was back in 1892. It was part of the Parish Day celebrations. Parish Day is still an annual event and has been since 1865. On the 1st June of that year a "Dedication Festival" was held upon the completion of the new South Transept in Byfleet Church. This was built by Henry Woodyer, an important Victorian architect but this is not a good example of his work. The whole parish was invited to lunch on the lawn of West Hall by the owner, Mr. R.H. Murray. Thus began the annual celebrations, initially with church services and lunch in the rectory garden but the parish soon varied this. The venue varied too and after 1885 so did the date. By that year too, "Dedication Festival" had given way to "Parish Day".

Opposite: Plane trees at West Hall
overhanging the canal above the grist mill.

THE EVER CHANGING SCENE

Murray's Lane, Conker Arch or Stoops' Drive are all local names for the track from Byfleet village to West Hall, crossing the canal at the next little bridge: Murray's Bridge. Their memory lives on. It was probably Stoops who planted the horse chestnut trees to create Conker Arch.

Above: Conker Arch, looking towards the canal, in August 1981

The first conker trees in the top scene were bulldozed out to make the M25 but the remainder show in the other two sketches. The lane now deviates to cross the bridge over the M25.

Opposition to the construction of the canal was just as great as for the motorway!

Above: The same view early in 1982
Below: Again at the end of the year.

34.

Mucking about
on the river
.....or in it !

After Murray's Bridge comes Dodd's Bridge and so down to Pyrford Lock through a calm meadow landscape with plenty of trees. Don't be surprised to spot Highland Cattle.

PYRFORD LOCK TO WALSHAM GATES

O.S. Map 187 : 054592 to 050578
Path Condition : Usually very good.

Once past the moorings this walk continues through scenes of trees and fields with the farmers acting out the cycle of their seasons. The fl and fauna are richer, the peace greater.

School Art Class
on the tow-path
Murray's Bridge.
1981

Pyrford Lock is very well known due to the popularity of 'The Anchor' which stands beside it. This is one of very few pubs which actually stand on the canal bank. People remember a real old country pub here, oil lamps and all.

The tow-path crosses the road and the road crosses the canal, by humping over the narrowest of bridges and doubling back on itself. Just watch the faces of unsuspecting motorists!

Past the moorings and the tow-path twists between trees. It shouldn't! Think what would happen to the tow-ropes! The tow-path used to run on the canal side but the canal has gradually shifted until now there is no room.

Next comes Pigeon House Bridge, beyond which a path on the left goes off to Ockham Mill. On the corner once stood stables and the black tar-boarded Pigeon House. The path to the Mill (dated 1862) was once the wagon route between the mill and the canal. Below the footbridge you can see the foundations in the river for a greater bridge for the wagons.

Maybe you won't expect to find an Egyptian sphynx nestling in the reeds where lawns come down to the water's edge but this is Pyrford Place and it has many a tale to tell.

When it was Crown property it was leased by Elizabeth I to her Latin secretary and greek scholar, Sir John Wolley. He had married one of the Queen's ladies-in-waiting, Elizabeth More, from Loseley, near Guildford. The Queen not only visited Loseley but she also came to stay here at Pyrford Place. Robert Dudley, Earl of Leicester, came too. It was he, in the presence of the Queen, who knighted Lady Wolley's father, here in the gardens of Pyrford Place.

29·10·1982

The stories continue. Sir John Wolley was succeeded by Francis Wolley and Lady Elizabeth took as her second husband Sir Thomas Egerton. It was a good choice as he later rose to be Lord Chancellor. Also expected to make a good match was her neice, Anne More, heiress to the Loseley estates. Instead she ran off and married Sir Thomas Egerton's secretary. He was John Donne whom we remember as a poet. This scandalous act put John Donne in the Fleet prison but now Sir Francis enters the story again. It was he who successfully reconciled the two families and had the Donnes come and live with him here at Pyrford.

Truth is never romantic enough for some people and I have been entertained with stories of Queen Elizabeth flirting with John Donne in the summerhouse!

The present summerhouse on the canal bank is late 17th C. but replaced an earlier one.

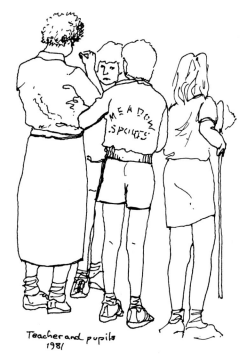

Teacher and pupils
1981

By Walsham Gates.
G. Howkins 1983

WALSHAM GATES:

To my way of thinking this is one of the most pleasant spots on the canal; quiet and peaceful out in the flood meadows of the Wey, approached by attractive country paths. Some come from Ripley, which claims to have the largest village green in England, although not all of it is recognisable as such. Other paths cross fields of vegetables. When the canal was built such fields, for feeding London, were at Battersea and Lambeth. By the late 18th C. they had been pushed out to Camberwell and Brixton. Now they seem a long way out.

Here also is another of the little footbridges (top). When they occur where the tow-path changes sides they are called 'turnover bridges'. Some books on our national waterways draw attention to there over the Wey, as an important part of our heritage.

The brickwork here is dated 1785.

Leek field
Walsham
1983

Mr. G. Bailey and his cottage
Walsham Gates. 1983.

Meet Mr. Bailey. All his life he has worked on the land. He knows it, he loves it and now, as agent for the National Trust, he cares for it. Without his guidance I should have missed interesting things on his stretch, from Pyrford to Newark, such as the hollows by the gateway to Walsham indicating where squatters once lived. Others lived in old railway trucks where the lock cottage garden is now. Evidently to get rid of the gypsies the trucks were set on fire. There and many other stories Mr. Bailey shares from his own wealth of oral history collected from visitors to Walsham, who tell him their memories from earlier days.

This device Mr. Bailey retrieved from a shed and restored in place. Explanation on next page.

Very special
see page 53 58

The
tow-path comes
down here with
the lock cottage
to the right. It
ends on a point of
land showing in the
bottom sketch. A footway
crosses the weir on the right
to begin as a tow-path again
along the bank from which the
bottom sketch was made.

The problem was to get barges across this wide pool as
they couldn't be towed across the top of the weir. A
post above the duck bears the pulley shown overleaf.
The tow-rope was threaded through this and then
hauled back on itself to propel the barge across the
pool under its own momentum. The rope was disconnected
at the crucial moment and taken with the horses
across the weir to be connected again when the
barge reached the other bank. Easy when you know how!
This system was used elsewhere, as at Weybridge
Lock to cross the pool there to enter the lock.
Punting poles assisted with downstream journeys.

The most important thing to notice at
Walsham gates is the lock itself.
Grass grows right down the banks into
the water. This is how all the locks
were originally built but now this is
the last surviving one.

Notice also the 'paddles' on the gates,
indicated with an arrow in the top
sketch on page 36 (4), and explained page 53 58

A third thing to note is that both
sets of gates are normally open. Only during
floods are there 'flood gates' closed.
Without them excess water would surge
into the canal, flooding places like New
Haw where the houses are below canal level.
When closed the water is forced over the
adjacent weir and along the River Wey
which separates from the canal here.
They rejoin at Weybridge Lock.
Water is always roaring and foaming
over the weir but to help imagine it in
spate there is a great raw basin beyond
the sluices, ripped out by the current.
This fills and overfills to inundate the
surrounding fields. This occurred so often
that a boat was kept at the cottage to
ferry the children across to school in
Ripley. Then in 1932 the depressed Welsh
were employed to cut a better channel.
Floods still occur though. The most
important job nowadays for the National
Trust employees is to act as Water
Controllers. They have no
less than twenty nine
sets of regulating gates
to attend.

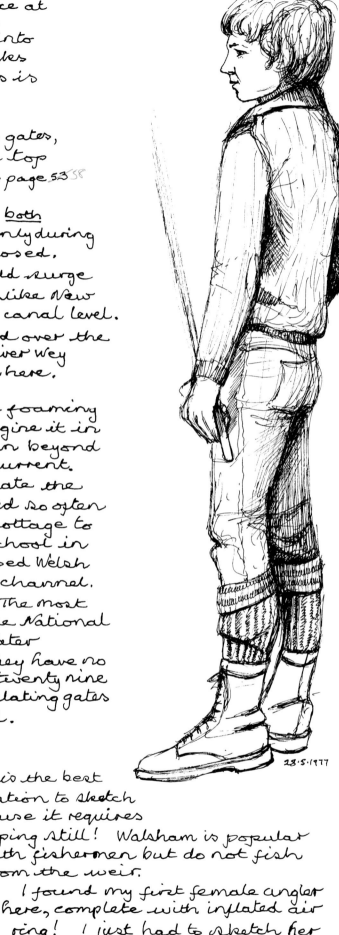

28.5.1977

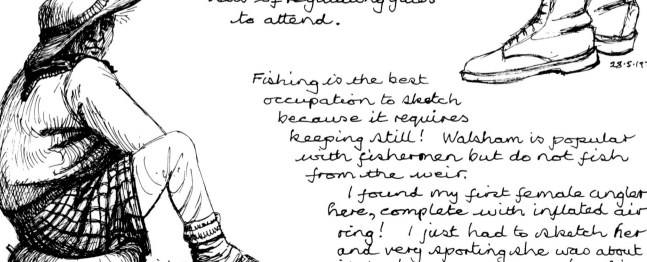

Fishing is the best
occupation to sketch
because it requires
keeping still! Walsham is popular
with fishermen but do not fish
from the weir.
I found my first female angler
here, complete with inflated air
ring! I just had to sketch her
and very sporting she was about
it too! She couldn't stop laughing
while I drew — so I told her I
would like to publish it !!

WALSHAM GATES
TO
NEWARK LOCK

O.S. Map 187 : 050578 to 042575 (on 186)

Path condition: through meadows; can be soft.

This is just a short walk through a couple of meadows. It's not so popular that the grass has been worn away so you might get your feet wet! There's not much to see, although the general scene is very attractive; a quiet place to relax and look out for birds and plants.

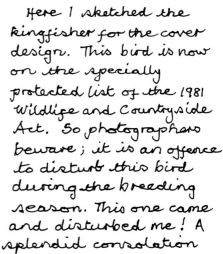

29·10·1982

Here I sketched the kingfisher for the cover design. This bird is now on the specially protected list of the 1981 Wildlife and Countryside Act. So photographers beware; it is an offence to disturb this bird during the breeding season. This one came and disturbed me! A splendid consolation for a cold wet day that made drawing difficult.

29·10·82

Must have gorged itself very heartily to be able to keep its balance at this angle.

C. Howkins 1982

Black-headed Gull in its summer plumage. It loses the black head in winter except for a spot behind the eye.

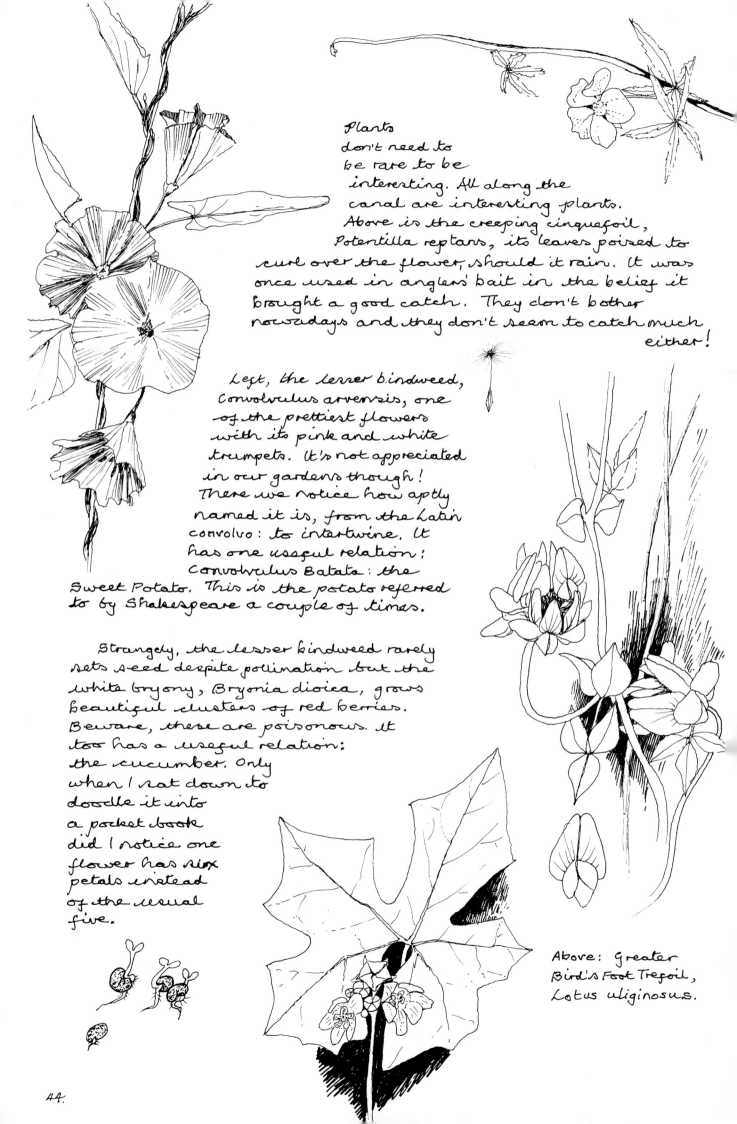

Plants
don't need to
be rare to be
interesting. All along the
canal are interesting plants.
Above is the creeping cinquefoil,
Potentilla reptans, its leaves poised to
curl over the flower, should it rain. It was
once used in anglers' bait in the belief it
brought a good catch. They don't bother
nowadays and they don't seem to catch much
either!

Left, the lesser bindweed,
Convolvulus arvensis, one
of the prettiest flowers
with its pink and white
trumpets. It's not appreciated
in our gardens though!
There we notice how aptly
named it is, from the Latin
convolvo: to intertwine. It
has one useful relation:
Convolvulus Batata: the
Sweet Potato. This is the potato referred
to by Shakespeare a couple of times.

Strangely, the lesser bindweed rarely
sets seed despite pollination but the
white bryony, Bryonia dioica, grows
beautiful clusters of red berries.
Beware, these are poisonous. It
too has a useful relation:
the cucumber. Only
when I sat down to
doodle it into
a pocket book
did I notice one
flower has six
petals instead
of the usual
five.

Above: Greater
Bird's Foot Trefoil,
Lotus uliginosus.

44.

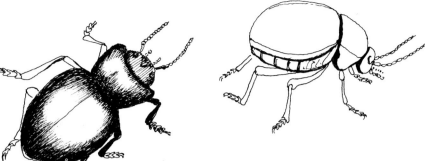

The damp vegetation
by the canal is
full of creepy-
crawlies!

Don't upset this chap;
it's got over 250 relatives
in Britain. It's a 'leaf
beetle' from the same
family as the famous Colorado
Beetle. I think this must have
been Melasoma populi but I'm not sure.

This is my favourite
beetle because it
frightens me to death.
It's a carnivore but
those jaws are not
supposed to be strong
enough to pierce
human skin. It did
not get chance to
try! I did not like
it invading my picnic
and it in return did
not like being
tricked into a
beaker for drawing.
So it arched its
abdomen like a
scorpion and
squirted stinking
yellow fluid
at me. Serves
me right I know.
It's a 'rove
beetle' and
has two splendid
names: Devil's
Coach Horse and
Ocypus olens.

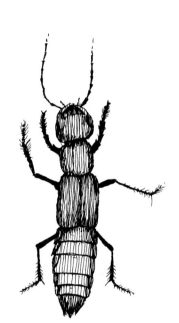

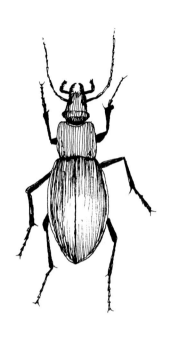

Above: the violet
ground beetle, Carabus
violaceus, is another
common beetle. It
has about 350
relatives in Britain.
In all there are
about 4,000 species
in our islands but
the text books don't
agree as to exactly
how many there
are.

These are all land
beetles. No doubt
there is a good
variety of water
beetles in the
canal itself.
I haven't been in
for a while!

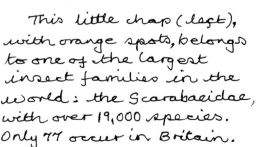

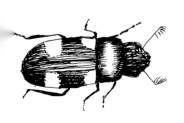

This little chap (left),
with orange spots, belongs
to one of the largest
insect families in the
world: the Scarabaeidae,
with over 19,000 species.
Only 77 occur in Britain.

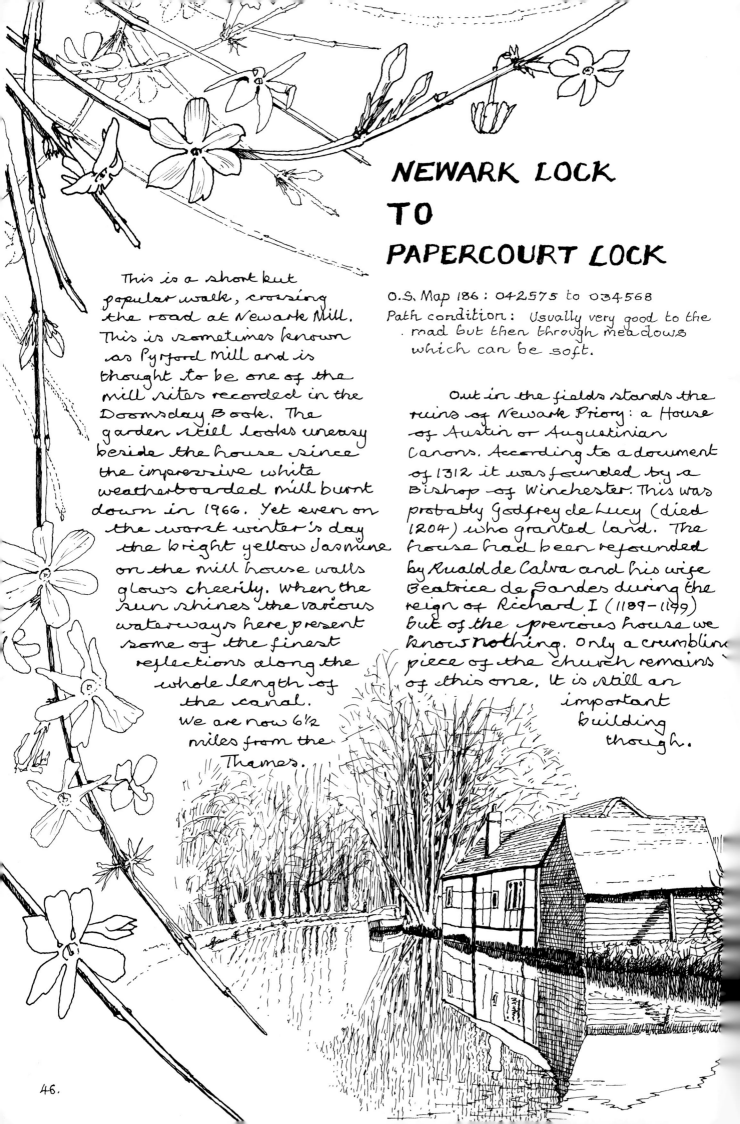

NEWARK LOCK TO PAPERCOURT LOCK

This is a short but popular walk, crossing the road at Newark Mill. This is sometimes known as Pyrford Mill and is thought to be one of the mill sites recorded in the Doomsday Book. The garden still looks uneasy beside the house since the impressive white weatherboarded mill burnt down in 1966. Yet even on the worst winter's day the bright yellow Jasmine on the mill house walls glows cheerily. When the sun shines the various waterways here present some of the finest reflections along the whole length of the canal.
We are now 6½ miles from the Thames.

O.S. Map 186 : 042575 to 034568
Path condition : Usually very good to the road but then through meadows which can be soft.

Out in the fields stands the ruins of Newark Priory: a House of Austin or Augustinian Canons. According to a document of 1312 it was founded by a Bishop of Winchester. This was probably Godfrey de Lucy (died 1204) who granted land. The house had been refounded by Ruald de Calva and his wife Beatrice de Sandes during the reign of Richard I (1189-1199) but of the previous house we know nothing. Only a crumbling piece of the church remains of this one. It is still an important building though.

Stories from the Priory are scant. I like the one about Canon John Chersterton who came unstuck in 1387 when charges were brought by the Bishop's Commission after a visitation. He was removed into the custody of Merton Priory for his 'excesses'. This leaves us to conclude that to sin in moderation was acceptable! Indeed this often seems to have been the case. Many medieval charges read 'too much', 'too many' or 'too often'. In this case the Prior, Alexander Culmeston, resigned too, supposedly infirm.

Among the disputes was the Prior's right to hold court and view of frank-pledge at Ripley. He also had the assize of bread and ale and view of frank-pledge at Puttenham. This was usually the sheriff's job but national practice varied greatly.

Life at the Priory has to be pieced together. After 1382 Saturdays must have been busy: serving an important chantry for John Newdigate and Laurentia, the widow of Peter atte Wode. At the Lady altar prayers were offered for the well being of Laurentia, the king and the bishop and for their souls after their deaths, together with Peter's soul. For this service a weekly payment of 7d was made from the endowment.

If February 10th fell on a Saturday they must have been especially busy because that was the date each year on which they prayed for the souls of their founders.

A visit from the Archbishop of Canterbury must have caused a bustle. John Peckham came several times, between 1281-3. I wonder if he came by water? The canons used the river as a highway.

Priory scenes reproduced from the Doorstep Book.

Mallard Pair,
Newark Priory
1978

47.

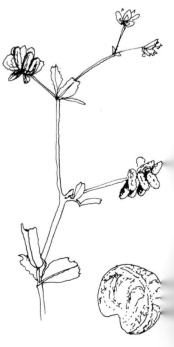

Right: Black Medick, one of our arable weeds. Its scientific name is Medicago lupulina. Try saying that fast! The fruits have a fascinating shape and pattern but the bright yellow flowers are tiny; only about 2mm. long. Bees find them though. The weight of the bees causes the flower to push forward its reproductive organs for pollination.

From Papercourt Lock a path runs through the above fields to Papercourt Farm. Here I recorded the young cattle in their shaggy winter coats. A little dark donkey is often with them, ("Herbie").

Lock Cottage is indicated in the background.

Previous page: Papercourt Farm, built in the 1660's, with richly coloured brick, when it was the Manor of Papworth. No doubt its predecessor was a half-timbered building. The name 'Papworth' was in existence in 1204, becoming 'Pappeworth' by the 14th C. and 'Papercourt' by 1686. It is not named as such in the Domesday Book (1086) but at Send reference is made to 1½ hides held by Walter and to 9 hides held by Herbert. One of these portions could have been Papworth. It is not even clear from whom these two held their lands.

The entry (no. XXXIII) says that Alfred of Marlborough held it from the King but that Reginald holds it from Alfred. However, at the beginning of the Book is recorded the list of landowners in Surrey. Here it is Reginald ('Rainaldus') son of Erchenbald who is listed, not Alfred.

In 1271 Ruald de Calva, the 'founder' of Newark Priory, granted it to the Weston family of West Clandon. It stayed in that family until the beginning of the 17th C. when Edmund Slyfield, Lord of West Clandon passed it to Henry Weston of Ockham. In 1711 John Weston sold it to Sir Peter King and its connection with the canal's founder was lost.

This page: Impatiens glandulifera or Giant Balsam; also known as Policeman's Helmet from the shape of the back of the flower, or Jumping Jack because its fruits explode and curl up when ripe. Press them between your finger and thumb when yellow and see; great fun! Introduced from the Himalayas in 1839 and is now widely naturalised, especially by waterways. It is only an annual but reaches seven feet; ten feet back in the Himalayas. It is common along the canal, often growing in 'thickets' to produce a beautiful show of bloom, from white to crimson, in summer.

Opposite: Grey Herons
Ardea cinerea.

B. Hawkins
1982

Fledgeling
Blackbird
in a Rowantree.
1982

PAPERCOURT LOCK
TO
WORSFOLD GATES

O.S. Map 186 : 034568 to 016557

Path Condition : Usually very good;
can be a little soft.
Gravel at Cartbridge.

After Papercourt the canal runs beside great open fields : green and quiet but which were not always so. This is the Broadmead. Here Henry VIII held tournaments for nearby was a royal manor used as a summer palace. Now it is reduced to rubble and fragments on private farmland.

The palace fell into decay after the Tudors and James I gave it for a small return to one of his foresters, Sir Edward Zouch.
Sir Edward pulled down the palace and used the materials to build Hoe Place up on the ridge above the water meadows. Hoe Place still exists but has been rebuilt.

Woking was a royal manor from the time of Edward the Confessor to Richard I from when it was leased out to Lords (Hollands, Keats, Somersets). Through the Somersets it was used by Margaret Beaufort before her son was crowned Henry VII. He was then able to give it to her. She, unlike him, made full use of it.

From here, her grandson, Henry VIII, frequently went hunting, fishing and jousting.
Here also his first wife, Catherine of Aragon, gave birth to Mary Tudor. I am assured modern research confirms this although history books record her birth at Greenwich.
Elizabeth visited here four times and Edward VI once.

Opposite : Tawny Owl

C. Hawkins 1983

Right:
  Cartbridge,
carrying the
A247 and the tow-
path over the canal;
the latest in a long
line of bridges here.

Below: looking back from
Papercourt Lock and sketched
from a photograph I took when the
          view seemed to capture the essence
                of the valley: the river-cum-canal
                  winding through the meadows, the
                    clumps and lines of trees, the tow-
                      path, the boats, the walkers
                        and fishermen, the
                          ponies and cattle.

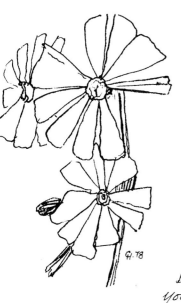

The tow-path doesn't really pass much to ponder over, except a large industrial building right on the canal edge. This is still known as the tannery but the actual tannery was burnt down. People remember the fire and the stink and that's about all.

Left: The tatty blooms of an out-of-season sprig of Red Campion.
Below: The Yellow Archangel or Galeobdolon. 'Gale' is Greek for weasel and 'bdolos' means a bad smell. I've never smelt a weasel so I'll just have to believe the greeks! Incidently, you have to crush a leaf to get the smell out.

Further on the far bank is lined with bamboo, rustling in the unfelt wind. It doesn't seem like England. I do not know which species it is. One plant, however, that is useful to know is our largest grass, the Common Reed, Phragmites communis. The bigger it is the wetter it is. So don't stray off the path. The man below did. In fact he tried to jump a wide band of quite luxuriant reed. He didn't so much land as immerse! His language was most unsuitable for a Sunday but high and dry on the towpath, we were much amused.

10·10·82

G. 1979

L. Hawkins 1982.

Worsfold Gates
Wey Navigation, Surrey.

WORSFOLD GATES
TO
TRIGGS LOCK

O.S. Map 186: 016557 to 013549

Path Condition: Good; through meadowland.

Right: In Worsfold gates the 'paddles' are very rare. They are often quoted as being the only survivors of an early system but this is not so. Another set survives downstream at Walsham Gates. So that you can find them their location is indicated on the drawing on page 36.41 The paddles are lifted and pinned in place rather than being wound up with a handle as is now universal.

CH.
9.8.1977

Previous page: Lock Cottage, Worsfold. The black weatherboarding seems out of character and reminds one more of Essex or Kent but it was once much used in Surrey, including on some of the canal-side buildings now gone. The notion of a timber frame clad in tarred boards began in Georgian times, around the S.E. coasts as a development from fishing boat construction. The idea spread widely inland and pitch gave way to the new and fashionable white lead paint. Newark Mill was a fine example. It also spread abroad to the Eastern United States, especially New England. Nowadays it has come back into fashion.

CH.
22.6.77

Send Church: the only rural medieval church really close to the canal. For a long way now the tow-path gives good views of the church and the scattered roof-tops of the village strung along the foot of a low ridge which raises them above the flood levels.

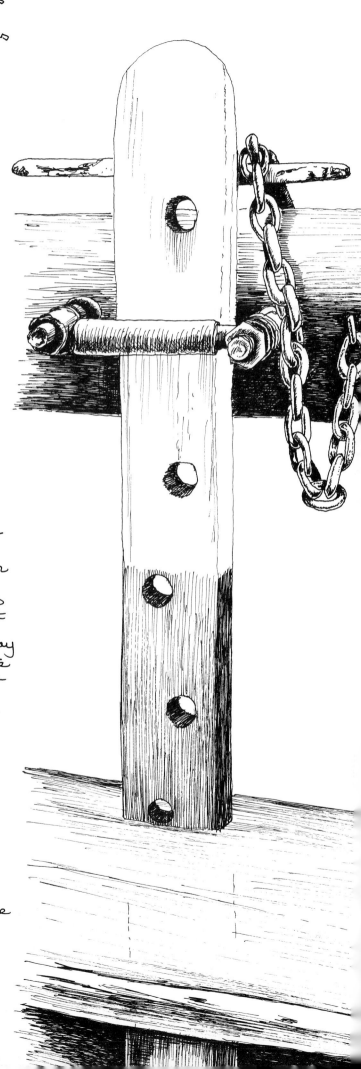

Worsfold Gates

The walk from Worsfold to Triggs is short but pleasant, from the landscape of the previous page out into the meadows again where the valley broadens. There's always something to catch the eye, whatever the season, such as these white rowing boats where the Wey rejoins the canal below Triggs Lock. They look simple enough but oh those curves! It was a beautiful day though. Weather doesn't matter. With the right materials one can even draw through showers but wind is enemy number one. It pushes and shoves and gets between the sketchbook pages however many bulldog clips you use. That happend on the previous page. It was beautiful when I drew the donkeys but when I moved round to the barges up got the wind. At least it gave opportunities to try and show the ripple pattern where it buffets the water. It happens so quickly though!

Puffballs; there are over 3,000 different fungi in Britain but the tow-path is not a good hunting ground as the humus layer is so thin. Those which feed on dead wood are the most plentiful.

TRIGGS LOCK
TO
BOWERS LOCK

O.S. Map 186: 013549
to 012529

Path Condition: Soon
after Triggs can be
soft and slippery
in winter and fields
near Bowers wet.
Long wet grass can
be found in summer.

✻ It skirts Sir Richard
Weston's park at
Sutton Place. This is
sometimes open to
the public. ✻

This is one of the longer
sections, being about two miles.
Soon after Triggs Lock there are no
access points along the route. It is
not one of the most interesting sections
in winter except for the all important point of it being so
rural and desolate yet with Guildford and Woking so very
close. In high summer it has all the beauty, fascination
and comfort of being truly English.

Moorhen

Coot

Triggs Lock is always a pleasant
spot. The river rejoins the canal
and a backwater rushes out; the
waters swirl into a lovely pool,
under the trees, below the lock.
The cottage was claimed by Harry
Stevens to have been his birthplace.
This is the man who in 1964,
shortly before his death, gave the
Wey Navigation to the National
Trust to safeguard for us all.
The family connection covers
three generations, from when
his grandfather took over the
management, followed by father
and son. This continuity brought
success after many changes of

ownership and the mis-
management of the Portmores
and Langtons. The Stevens family
was able to buy the canal
themselves in 1902 and their
name can be seen on the
barges featured in so many of
the old photographs. This lasted
until 1958 when regular traffic
to Guildford ceased.

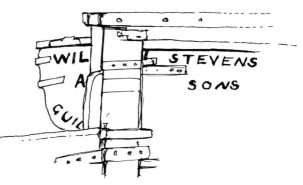

WIL
A
GUI
STEVENS
SONS

BOWERS LOCK TO STOKE LOCK

O.S. Map 186
012529 to 002516

Path Condition: usually good. Parts can be soft.

H.
6·4·83

Take a look at a map and you'll imagine that the surrounding built-up areas will have marred this stretch. You'll be wrong. It's one of the most attractive. Winding curves keep you full of anticipation as to what's round the next bend. The broad fields of the previous stretch change to smaller more intimate water meadows, some boggy and rich in wildlife. The trees close in, enriching the range of flora and birds, and blocking some of the views to keep you guessing as to what really does lie ahead. If you brave the winter you'll find snowdrops. The first warmth brings the celandines and white violets and, for the sharp-eyed, the moschatel. Then the Lady's smock and so into the richness of summer until the floating leaves burnish the water and the alder catkins once again turn over to hang through the cold.

Stoke
Lock.

Celandines

Stoke
Lock is the
earliest pound lock
in Surrey and claimed
also as earliest in England
but it is not clear from early
records of other canalisations
whether this type of pound lock was used. Almost certainly it was.
Originally it was part of three miles of canal built by Sir Richard
Weston during 1618-19 in his estate of Sutton Place. It was not for
transport but for irrigation and flood control as part of his
experiments to improve the agriculture on his estates. From this
developed the idea of canalising the Wey right down from
Guildford. The actual lock structure we see today is not
of course the original. Centuries of maintenance have
obliterated that.

If we had to list typically English scenes would we
not include the image of pollarded willows along
a river bank in open meadowland? Here they
are. The scene below is looking downstream from Stoke Lock. Opposite
is the other end of the
line, looking upstream
from the
Bowers
end.

Stoke Lock reminds me of a winter's afternoon when I went to visit Mr. Stephen White. The snow was gleaming on the Downs outside but warm and snug in his lounge he recalled for me his life on the canal, from 1920 until he was the last bargee and retired, in 1968. His father had worked the Basingstoke Canal. His grandfather had worked the Wey Arun Canal. Carefully going through his large collection of photographs he brought it all to life again with a clarity and vigour that concealed his age.

It became very clear that we were not just talking about shifting barges up and down a canal.

Watermills and windmills and looms can be specially run to satisfy our curiosities but there was so much more to a canal that the running of tourist barges would not even echo. It was a tough arduous way of life linking so many different interests in the Surrey way of life. That way of life has gone and the canal now serves different needs.

I asked Mr. White to describe a typical journey. Here is that description, transcribed from the tape recording made that afternoon. Only the punctuation has been added.

Mr. Stephen White:

" We would start from Stoke Lock. We'd start from there somewhere about five. We'd push the barge down to Bowers Lock and then the horses would catch us up; one horse or two horses... Then we get onto the Thames. We'd bow-haul or push them or row them down to Teddington, carry on through into London, p'raps go into a dock or into a wharf and may take any-thing from a week to a month to get a full load. Well then you'd come out of the dock. Then you'd row up to Putney. You'd pick up a horse there. He'd pull you up to wherever you were going. The latter years, say from 1920-1, you'd have a horse down, most probably from Guildford, pull you to Weybridge. You'd carry on from Weybridge, down to Putney with the horse and then sail or row your barge from there to London and as time went on you'd have a small tug back up from the docks up to Teddington or Weybridge and the first one I can remember was a tug called The Indian Chief; very noisy tug, and then as time went on you'd have a larger tug. They'd pick you up at Weybridge somewhere about midday or late or early afternoon. You'd go down to Kingston and perhaps wait till next morning till the next tide which most probably at 2 or 3 o'clock in the morning. Then you'd carry on into London and probably go to a wharf, load, and tow back out with a, what we used to call, a London Tug and then perhaps when we go to Brentford or Teddington you'd have a tug that would be called "up country" or "river tug". Well the journey then from Kingston to Weybridge used to take about 2½ hrs. and then the horses would pick you up at Weybridge, take you to Coxes. You'd unload about 25 ton at Coxes and carry on up river till dark and then carry on the next morning as soon as it was daylight and stop somewhere up the river for breakfast. That's all. Then, most probably if you had a lot of work, you'd discharge that night and you'd carry on and you wouldn't even have time to go home and get clean clothes.....

A barge jack

.... Sometimes, sometimes you'd go into London, if you maybe wanted urgently into London; ships waiting there or ships coming in early and p'r'aps your freight is supposed to be first from the ship. .... and maybe turned out to be the bottom of the ship where you may lay there from a week to three weeks for your trip for your cargo. And another, you go in and can do a freight in 48 hrs. No sleep. I've laid in the dock waiting for timber; p'r'aps a Canadian ship; perhaps in her lower hold, in what is called "the tanks" she had wheat, Canadian wheat. Well, before you can get to that you have to unload all the timber, Canadian timber; about three weeks. No money coming in. So, as I said, what I used to do then, I used to get in touch with different people to navigate some of the passenger vessels, Not very often. Had one or two in London. Not supposed to."

(Not edited)

A barge kettle that slotted into the rocking stove for safety.

STOKE
LOCK
TO
MILL MEAD
LOCK

O.S. Map 186 : 002516 to 996492

Path Condition :

    Stoke Lock to Stoke Bridge - good
    Stoke Bridge to Bye-pass Bridge -
        can be soft.
    Bye-pass Bridge to Dapdune -
        good ; long wet grass in summer.

N.B. Just past Dapdune is a waterlogged patch.
    Dapdune to Town Centre - good but
        beware long wet grass in summer.
    Town Centre - hard surface.

Route : <u>Stoke Bridge</u> is a turnover bridge -
continue from far left of parapet.
<u>By</u>-pass Bridge (old A3) - the main
road has to be crossed.
Continue from right hand end.

<u>Dapdune</u> : If your footwear won't let
you through the wet use road from
railway viaduct or cross canal by
footbridge on viaduct, turn right at
main road and so onto town centre.

<u>Town centre</u> : where the paving begins
head straight for the church tower
beside which the tow-path begins
again.

The church is St. Nicholas', shown
above. It was rebuilt 1875 but
retains the 15thC. Loseley Chapel
and monuments to some of the
More family.

Despite penetrating into
the heart of the town
this stretch is still varied.
To anyone who is interested
in seeing the development
of Guildford this is in fact
quite rewarding. It does
not give a complete picture
of the town's development
because the Priory and
Royal Park each side of
the river prevented early
development and the later
development has been
largely ripped out and
rebuilt in recent times.

Stoke Lock is
surprising because it is
high above the flood plain
and swirling river. When
these meadows flood it
is a good place for bird-
watching, to see what
has joined the gulls
in scavenging for the
drowned beasties.

By Stoke Bridge is a pub called "The Row Barge". Oddly, this seems to be the only obvious commemoration of canal life.

Eleven pubs are said to have served the canal. Only five (?) stand on the waterside, including The Anchor at Pyrford.

The name 'Anchor' probably comes from the 'anker': a unit of measurement of drink.

Stoke Bridge (below) is a County Council job of 1926. The mill is the grandest piece of Victoriana along the path. There is a long tradition of milling at Stoke but it is always difficult to differentiate the mills because "mills" in old records does not mean buildings but the waterwheels or grinding stones. Thus a site or district may have more than one mill without having more than one building. Milling doesn't necessarily imply corn either. There were corn mills at Stoke but there were paper mills as well. Whatever the product, millers and bargees do not happily co-exist. The working of locks reduces the water and the pressure available to millers. This caused endless disputes, especially where the river worked the mills before canalisation. Bargees often had to pay the miller for the water. This was the case at Stoke. New mills after canalisation had their terms set out by the Navigation authorities. Here at Stoke a policy called "The Millers' Indenture" was agreed in 1832, settling the working of this as well as the Newark and Woking mills. Weybridge followed in 1849.

If the water dispute seems trivial it was not. In 1794 Guildford raised £124.12s.6d from charging 1d per load at the wharf. That means there were 29,910 loads.

Guildford Cathedral: planned in 1534 but not begun until 1936 and consecrated in 1961. There on Stag Hill it makes an eye-catching feature from so many directions; so it should.

This silhouette was sketched from the tow-path opposite Dapdune Wharf. A more interesting view, showing its dominance over the city can be seen from the path back near Stoke Bridge, looking across the meadows. To the right can easily be read the name 'Dennis' across the largest factory. It moved here in 1905, originally for car production but was given over in 1913 to producing large public vehicles. The Dennis brothers, Raymond and John, had moved to Guildford from Devon in 1895 and began their business with bicycles.

Below: a barge weight.
These were used to weigh the loads.

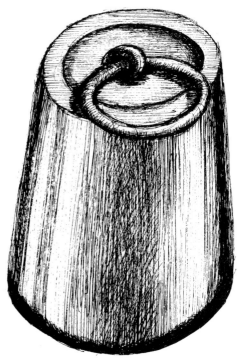

By Dapdune Wharf is a rather splendid brick viaduct. This was built in 1885 by the London and South Western Railway to carry their line from Guildford to Hampton Court. Other beautiful brick arched viaducts can be seen in the Mole Valley at Leatherhead and Dorking. Here at Guildford the main line from London arrived in 1845.

Opposite: Dapdune Wharf from the towpath. Lovely Surrey tile and brick, overhanging trees and lush vegetation make this scene appear so rural and yet you can hear the city centre right behind it. Once this spot was a very busy site, building barges etc. The last barge built on the Wey left here in 1965.

Left: Dapdune Wharf from the City side (reached from Wharf Road off Woodbridge Road, by the Y.M.C.A. building).

Leaving the pavement beside all the traffic it's quite astonishing to find this unpretentious nook and to sit among the grasshoppers and wild flowers to draw the scene in the low warm sun of an October afternoon.

The nearest part of the building is the Wharf Cottage with the wharfinger's cottage on the other end. The far roof sheltered carbide during the First World War.

It's all known busy industrial days, not just as a wharf but as a centre for barge building. It's easy to overlook how complex it is to build a barge. Here there were men working at the saw pits, others at steam bending; marvellous scenes to sketch. Romantic to draw — gruelling to work.

Left: a building on the new waterfront in city centre. This crane was moved here for preservation when the centre was rebuilt. It was operated by men walking a tread-wheel inside the building. It seems unbelievable now but it was still working this way in living memory.

This highlights one of the problems of recording remembered history. When was it last used. The date 1908 is given but Mr. White (see p 59.) remembers treading it and he did not begin work on the canal until 1920. It is also said to have been used last for lifting stone for the Cathedral. That began in 1936. Mr. White doesn't remember that. I've given up asking! It seems more important to gaze through the railings at the great wheel, eighteen feet in diameter, and imagine men treading it, whoever they were. History is about people, not dates.

Nowadays, pigeons seem to like it; descendants from those kept for food back in the Middle Ages.

GUILDFORD has been an important place since Anglo-Saxon times when King Alfred bequeathed it to his nephew. There was a mint here by 978 so it was already a borough and such an important place would need defending. It is much argued whether the castle mound is entirely Norman or whether it is a strengthening of earlier defences. Nearby, the church of St. Mary still stands, showing us its Saxon origins. The town grew up around these two, enhanced by the royal palace adjacent to the keep. The keep remains; the palace has gone and so has the Dominican Friary. The royal lands and the Friary lands restricted the development of the town and helped dictate the shape and pattern of the Guildford we have now, hundreds of years later.

72.

There is much to see which illustrates this long heritage despite its modern history being dominated by enormous redevelopment to increase the shopping facilities. Trade has always been vital. In the Middle Ages wool was all important. When that trade declined Weston promoted his canal idea to revitalise it and thereby won essential support from the townsfolk. Back in 1614, George Abbot, Archbishop of Canterbury and native of Guildford, made his first attempt to revive the wool trade. Eventually he set up workshops but they failed. The wool trade died. The canal found other cargoes much needed by the traders and townsfolk. The people keep Guildford alive and add to its history through their needs and greeds and generosities, their education and religion, prejudices and fashions. There may be little to draw along the canal but all the people are an endless fascination.

73.

Castle Keep c. 1170
17·10·82

SKETCHING

AROUND

GUILDFORD

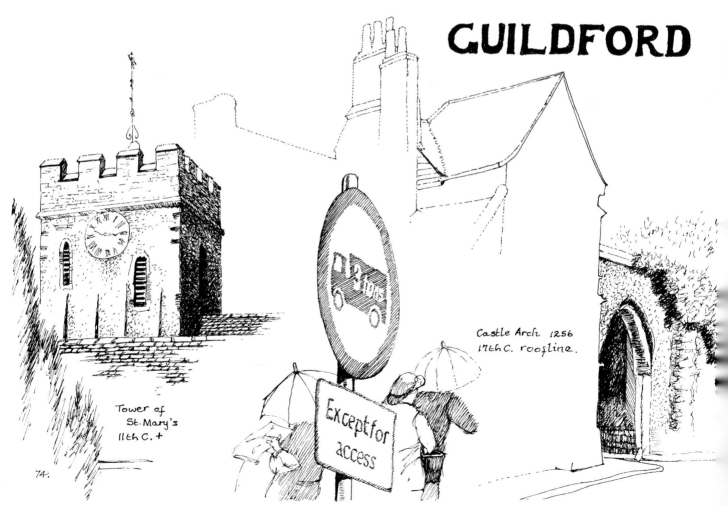

Tower of
St. Mary's
11th C. +

Except for
access

Castle Arch 1256
17th C. roofline.

74.

Left: "The Valley" 1891
Below: "Rosemary Alley"
Below left: "The Chestnuts" where Lewis
    Carroll died in 1898, and
    (centre) detail from gate pier, 1932.

Guildford: Town Mill 1770+
G. Hawkins 1982/3.

Opposite: Town Mill and mill pond used by canoeists where, in the 18th C. fish were farmed. The mill looks of one age but several rebuildings have been very skilfully matched. The date 1896 on the side doesn't refer to the walls but to the installation of new water pumps soon after Guildford Corporation took over the building as a pumping station. This had already been part of its business since the 18th C. Corn milling was its chief use until then, as with other mills at Guildford, now gone. They also served as "fulling" mills; cleaning and fluffing-up the famous woollen cloth.

Some of this was dried on racks in the field on the south bank: the mill mead.

Town Mill was bought by Henry Smith in 1624 and through him the income went to relieve the Guildford poor. This obviously suited the Corporation very well. Thus in 1665 they ordered that all local clothiers and mealmen must use the Town Mill!

The first records date from the early 13th C. although the town must have had mills since Saxon times. So why were they omitted from the Domesday tax return?

23·6·83
Fledgling Blackbird

MILLMEAD
TO
ST. CATHERINE'S LOCK

Above: looking from the tow-path to St. Catherine's Chapel when the adjoining flood meadows have been inundated, leaving the canal bank as a causeway.

O.S. Map 186 : 996492 to 996477

Path Condition : Usually good except after floods.

Now the GODALMING NAVIGATION

This is a short stretch but a surprising one for leaving the city behind so rapidly. So soon one is under the trees, and the best (?) spot on the canal to enjoy autumn colours. The drooping branches of the beeches shed a thick layer of floating gold on the water, to be curled back by the wake of a boat, like a scene in a giant creamery.

The boats are still important. Their licences contribute a major part to the maintenance bill for the canal, running at some £100,000 per annum. Over 1,000 non-powered boat licences are issued each year, plus 18 licences for each of the two commercial boathouses, plus all the private craft and the two "tripping" boats. The "trippers" amount to about 30,000 a year. Harry Stevens has one of the boats named after him.

Shrew
9.4.80

78.

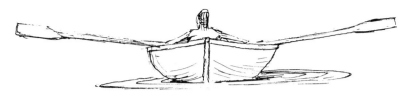

The waters bite deeply into St. Catherine's Hill. A lane comes down to the tow-path. This is the "Pilgrims' Way", the "Strata de Geldone" of the earliest record (1189). The 'Pilgrims' Cottage' dates from the 16th C but with 18th C. work showing too. Here was a ferry until 1964 and now there are plans for a footbridge over the water so that the North Downs Way can follow the traditional route. In the chapel here, prayers were offered for a safe crossing, or thanks given for having had one. A sister chapel, St. Martha: stands on the opposite hill. The two saints are said to have shared a hammer when building their chapels, and tossed it to each other across the valley; no doubt with loud warnings of "Coming over!"

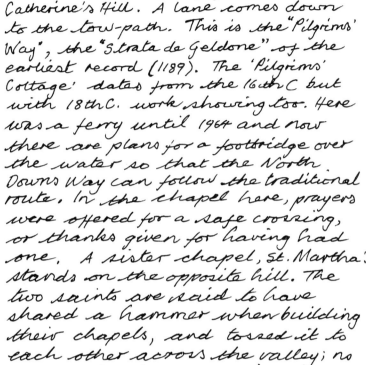

Cries of a different kind are also silenced between book covers : cries from St. Catherine's Fair. History records how rowdy it was and Turner has recorded what it looked like, with the booths on the hillside facing Guildford. His picture was published as an engraving in 1832.

John Bunyan's association with Shalford opposite has led to the suggestion that his Vanity Fair in 'Pilgrim's Progress' is based upon this fair.

Now it's a peaceful spot to enjoy views up and down the valley.

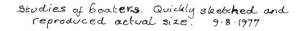

Studies of boaters. Quickly sketched and reproduced actual size. 9.8.1977

Another view of the flooded water meadows. This time from St. Catherine's Hill looking downstream to the castle. Heavy rains are a great worry to The National Trust who are liable to be blamed for any flooding. The main catchment area of the River Wey is about 30 miles x 35 miles and the rains are fed into the river by some 182 tributaries. Only in the final stages does it come under Trust control, when it has gathered all its power and when its only option is to continue down its valley. Some pressure can be reduced by opening some sluices to increase the rate of flow. Other sluices release extra water into the side channels but all that water has to return to the main course eventually. Further water can be released into flood meadows, such as this one at Guildford. If all that fails so does the weakest point. The last severe flooding was in September 1968 when six inches of rain fell in a few hours. Stoke Mill impeded the flow and the backup inundated the lower streets of Guildford. 1975 and 1979 were bad years too. Fortunately the situation is constantly monitored by six water-controllers for The National Trust plus extra help from private landowners. Thus floods are unusual but this only encourages the development of the natural flood plain. Should this increase so will the risk of flooding.

Beside
'The Pilgrims' Way'

St. Catherine's
Chapel

Built in 1317.

It is now a ruin, grey and brooding on its hilltop or shining gold and white in the sunlight. Imagine the rubble newly plastered over, put back the window tracery and roof, raise up the soaring pinnacles and the corner turret, add a fresh coat of whitewash and what a gleaming gem this must have been. Even now we can see inside where the processions passed but it's a pity the Victorians called the prehistoric road 'The Pilgrims' Way'. It closes out minds to all the other travellers. If we must be romantic remember also the crusaders, the royal hunting parties, the wealthy cloth merchants and the poor sheep drovers, the foreign envoys and the strange smells lingering after the passing spice merchants.

Let us also remember the drudgery of the miles of mud, remember the motives for some of the pilgrimages and the suffering of the penitents in bare feet, remember the poverty danger and distress all along the road.

Look down on the village of Shalford, associated with John Bunyan and remember the journey in 'Pilgrim's Progress'.

If you must be romantic, look further upstream to Peasmarsh, to one of the sites suggested for King Arthur's Astolat.

medieval travellers.

81.

ST. CATHERINE'S LOCK
TO
UNSTEAD LOCK

Looking downstream from St. Catherine's Lock to the ruined chapel on the skyline.

O.S. Map 186 : 996477 to 992460

Path Condition : Meadows can be waterlogged.

The first stretch, down to Broadford Bridge (A248) is mostly through open meadows, very pleasant if not waterlogged but exposed to the chill winter winds.

The lock cottage, which is not original is set back from the lock, where the Wey branches from the canal. No longer is the canal the Wey Navigation but the Godalming Navigation. It stretches four miles from Millmead to Godalming Wharf, has four locks and falls only thirty two feet. The Act of Parliament was passed in 1760 and the canal opened four years later: slow progress compared with the Wey Navigation.

The Commissioners passed it to the National Trust on 7th May 1968 through the Godalming and Guildford Corporations.

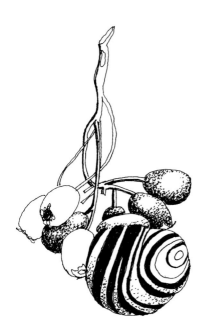

6·11·82
Broadford

The Godalming Navigation traded heavily in the timber from the south and west of Godalming. There was iron there too, coming not only from nearby Milford but from right down to the Hindhead Hills aswell. Barrels became important; oak for the staves, iron for the hoops. However there were other important timber loads, from planks to bark for tanning. Flour, paper and finished iron were also regular loads.

Looking upstream to Broadford Bridge.

Broadford Bridge is an area of great interest and a lot of variety, not all of which is immediately apparent. It is also an area to watch with interest in the next few years as the National Trust are hoping to be able to make improvements here as they own some of the adjoining land.

Looking upstream from Broadford Bridge. Rain stopped play!

— 83.

Just up from Broadford Bridge the canal branches directly away from you, as shown in the sketch above. This is known as the Gun's Mouth and is the former entrance to the Wey and Arun Junction Canal. Here is Stonebridge Wharf but the canal only penetrates as far as you can see. It can be approached from the other side from where the A281 crosses a bridge south of Shalford. A concealed footpath runs from the end of the bridge. (O.S. Map 186 : 000464).

The Act of Parliament for the Wey and Arun Junction Canal was passed in 1813 and it was opened in 1816. It is 18½ or 23 miles to the Arun depending how you view the other end when they are side by side.* A society with over 900 members is planning to restore it.

In 1871 it closed after many problems. A major problem was water because the canal falls in both directions from its highest point; 48 feet to the Wey and 122 feet to the Arun. Potentially it was a profitable venture as it linked London with the South Coast. The opening of the railway brought almost instant death.

See page 82.

* The River Arun and the canal run side by side!

84.

Behind the wharf and visible through the trees from the tow-
path is this weatherboarded barn raised on staddle stones.
It is not in its original position and may be moved again
yet, if the National Trust do get the chance to improve the site.
This humble little building gets so much attention because
it's the last gunpowder store to survive on the wharf.

Nearby runs the River Tillingbourne and for hundreds of
years the lower valley was a centre for making gunpowder.
Back in 1625 the East India Company set up mills at
Chilworth but there were probably not the first. A new
lease of life began in 1885 when the Chilworth Gunpowder
Company was formed. Production of a full range of
different powders continued to be made until 1920 when
the site finally closed. It stretched for about two miles
and quite a number of buildings and other surface
features still survive.

The gunpowder was brought down to Stonebridge Wharf for
transporting on the canal. I am told the barges used
for this had a red warning line painted around them
and that while loading a red flag was flown.

Field Notes from a pocket book :-

Coots which usually prefer more
open water and so are
scarcer than moorhens on
the canal.

Hedgehog drawn under a street
light (can't miss opportunities!).

Two Views of
Wharf Cottage
Probably once the Wharfinger's
Cottage.

Leaving the Gun's Mouth behind, the tow-path crosses meadowland towards a former railway embankment. This was the line from Guildford to Horsham.

cattle

It was very scenic but became unprofitable and was closed down on June 12th 1965. Thus it didn't quite make its centenary, having opened on October 2nd 1865. It was then run by the London, Brighton and South Coast Railway Company. Within two years it was putting the Wey and Arun Junction Canal out of business and the Act for closing the canal went before Parliament. One of its chief cargoes was coal from the south coast ports and the railway soon showed it could transport this quicker and cheaper. Other cargoes were mainly corn, chalk for agricultural lime and timber for London.

Field sketches of pheasants.

6·6·83

Nowadays the scenes are usually quietly rural with peace to study the rounded bodies of young cattle or to creep up on the pheasants, to note the yellow-green of the osier catkins in spring or the deep gold of the marsh marigolds. There are soon plenty of trees and so a wide variety of birds.

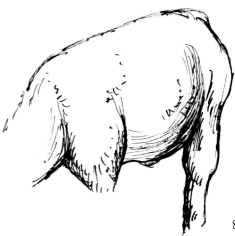

Cattle studies above Broadford. 1979

UNSTEAD LOCK
TO
CATTESHALL LOCK

O.S. Map 186 : 992460 to 980445

Path Condition: Good

   The rural walk continues: a beautiful harmony
of trees and fields and low wooded hills. It is
perhaps the richest stretch for the variety of wild
flowers, making a July walk very memorable.
Most beautiful are the dark blue damsel flies,
Agrion splendens, with dark blotched wings.
   The historic past does not draw attention
to itself along here.

Before leaving Unstead behind imagine
water mills again. Take yourself inside
and have a look around.
   In 1899 in Unstead Mill you would
have seen:-

6 pairs of stones
6 pairs of reduction rolls
7 pairs of granulation rolls
Armfield's Patent Centrifugal Sifter
2 smutters for wheat cleaning
Smith's Patent Centrifugal Dressing Machine
4 other dressing machines
2 purifiers
"Koh-i-Noor" sifter
2 separating reels
Large double centrifugal dressing machine
Double rotary plansifter
Wheat washing tackle
2 bran sifters
4 Van Gilder's Separators
Oat crusher
Large chaff cutter
6 sets of hoisting tackle
Powerful beam engine
2 large iron-framed water wheels.

Did you imagine all that?!

From Sales Catalogue, courtesy of
   Guildford Museum.

Rabbits: mixed ages. 6·6·83
Field notes in felt tip pen.
Reproduced actual size.

CATTESHALL

From the rural countryside one suddenly arrives at Catteshall and it's usually a busy spot, with many people attracted to Farncombe Boathouse. From Trowers Bridge there have been houses with big gardens but it's still been a gentle scene. On their other side, however, traffic thunders along the main Guildford to Godalming road (A3100). I bet they miss the lovely old Wyatt Almshouses (1622) set back towards the canal.

Catteshall is an odd little development: part industrial, part residential. It's worth a nose around at a quiet moment if you like that sort of thing.

An old black and white timbered house shows that this spot is older than it seems and no doubt has a tale to tell....

There are 12th C. references to Cateshull and Chatishull when it was a manor and tithing of Godalming. Henry I granted it to Oyrus Purcell. His son, Geoffrey, was the king's usher of the chamber. That means he was responsible for the linen and the laundresses. Perhaps it was too much for him for he retreated to the famous abbey at Reading to be a monk. He gave Catteshall to the Abbey.

Just up from the lock is the mouth to a backwater. Here long boats have to turn around and finish their last few yards in reverse, to the wharf at Godalming (shown below).

Opposite: Godalming Church and bowling green from the riverside walkway.

C. Howkins 1982/3

Godalming, Surrey.
S. Howkins 1982-3

GODALMING
Wharf is not much more than a mooring place nowadays and not especially attractive. Conscious of this, The National Trust, who own the adjoining land, will have the opportunity to demolish some of the existing old buildings and landscape the site. In the next few years they plan to do just that.

Godalming, like Guildford, deserves a book to itself it's such a fascinating old town. One walk is to go into town from the bridge and find the interesting old buildings. Look above the shop fronts. Explore the side streets too. It all gets better the further you go in: up to "the Pepperpot" (Market Hall, 1814) and down Church Street and even further on into Mill Lane, Mint Street, etc.

Alternatively, from the bridge, walk beside the river through the fields (The Burys) up to the church. These are the old Lammas lands from the days of common fields and communal farming. Fortunately they are preserved. Often they have cattle in them as of old and even a gaggle of geese when I went sketching - just like the Victorian paintings of Surrey.

Above: Geese on the Lammas Land. Sketched from the Burys.

Below: The same spot ten minutes later. Cattle right next to the heart of the town, as for hundreds of years. Let's keep it that way.

Opposite: Junction of Church Street with High Street, with the Pepperpot and a double over-sailed building - rare in Surrey.

The tow-path has taken us through lands that have been modified by man since prehistoric times. There is no virgin land left in Surrey.

On this journey we have 'met' many people who's names are familiar to us for the part they played in our national history. Surrey has always been an important place.

Here at Godalming we meet a new landowner in the story, the bishop of Salisbury. He aquired the manor in 1221 and his successors held it until 1541.

Long before that King Alfred held it and passed it on to his nephew Ethelwald. He died in a rebellion against Edward the Elder in 905.

Other important holders include Edward the Confessor and William de Warenne.

Finally we must recall the Mores of Loseley again. It became theirs in 1601 and they kept it for over two and a half centuries.

Mr. B.O. Ratcliffe MABEE is the man with the difficult job of managing the Navigations for us. They are an odd property for stretching some twenty miles but being only about one chain (66ft) wide. He also has to maintain good relations with all the other groups involved from adjoining landowners to the Water Authorities. He is even 'Admiral' of a fleet of twelve maintenance craft. There are twenty four bridges to safe-guard too and all the locks. The lock walls are eight to ten feet thick but the gates are less robust. Two to four new pairs are made each year (£1500 a gate) at the Maintenance yard at Send. Getting the old out and the new ones in is quite a job. So's the whole business but thank you for doing it.

ACKNOWLEDGEMENTS

Most of the information has been collected orally and to all the people who have helped, I am very grateful. In particular Mr. H. Cook of Byfleet and Mr. T. Harding of Old Woking gave up evenings to pass on their knowledge which I much appreciated. Lots of strangers passed on snippets when they met me drawing and these have been just as valuable.

Mr. B. Ratcliffe, Manager of the Navigations for The National Trust, and his agent, Mr. G. Bailey, also gave a lot of their time and knowledge. Thanks.

The staff at the Museums of Chertsey, Guildford and Weybridge were extremely helpful and encouraging, making the task so much easier and more enjoyable.

Thank you also to Mr. S. White of Guildford for the benefit of his memories of working the canal.

My thanks are also due to Miss Anne Bawtree for proof reading, to Mrs. Anne Searle for her criticisms of the illustrations, to Robert Hall for ruling up thousands of pencil lines on the manuscript pages and to his parents for rubbing them all out again afterwards.

SOURCES

The oral information has been verified wherever possible at the Museums acknowledged above. They also provided documentary material. Weybridge Museum has a permanent display and a useful booklet: "The Wey Navigation – a Tale of Troubled Waters" by Avril Lansdell. Guildford Museum has a large display and a scale model of "Perseverance IV" which can be seen by arrangement.

A full history of the Navigations has not yet been produced.